Experiences Unpacked:
A Short Story Collective
The TNT Group

Prelude

Thanks for purchasing or reading *'Unpacking Experiences'*: A handbook for English as second language learners, teenagers, and advanced kids'. This book is designed to help young learners improve their understanding of the English language while also gaining valuable insights into the complex world of personality traits and life lessons. Through engaging stories and relatable characters, this book will navigate learners on a journey of self-discovery, helping them to better understand themselves and the people around them.

From understanding the different personality traits and how they shape our interactions with others, to learning valuable life lessons and coping strategies for dealing with difficult situations, this book is packed with information and insights that will help learners navigate the challenges of growing up.

Whether you're an English as a second language learner, a teenager, or an advanced kid, this book is the perfect tool for developing your language skills and gaining a deeper understanding of yourself and the world around you. So let's begin our journey together and discover the secrets of personality traits and life lessons that will help you succeed in today's fast-paced world.

Timmy did not enjoy reading however his parents and teachers tried to encourage him to read, but he still found it boring and difficult.

One day, Timmy's class went on a field trip to the city library. At first, Timmy was not excited to be there, but as he wandered through the stacks, he stumbled upon a book that caught his eye. It was about a group of friends who went on an adventure to find a lost treasure. Timmy was hooked from the first page.

As he read the book, Timmy discovered that reading was not boring at all. It was exciting and opened up a whole new world of possibilities. He realized that through reading, he could learn about different cultures, places, and time periods. He could also learn new words and improve his vocabulary.

Timmy's reading skills improved, and he found that he was able to understand and enjoy other subjects in school more easily. He also found that he was able to express himself better in writing and speaking.

From then on, Timmy made a point to read every day. He even started a book club with his friends. He discovered that reading was not just important for his education, but also for his personal growth and enjoyment.

And so, Timmy became a lifelong lover of reading, and his parents and teachers were proud of the change they saw in him.

Mary was always in a hurry rushing through her homework, scarfing down meals, and even rushing through playing with her friends. His parents tried to teach her the importance of patience, but Mary just couldn't seem to slow down.

Mary's father took her to a farm to teach her a lesson in patience. The farmer showed them all around, and Mary was fascinated by the animals and the crops. But when the farmer took out a handful of seeds to show them how to plant them, Mary grew impatient. "Can we just plant them already?" she said. The farmer smiled and said, "Patience is key when planting. You have to take your time and be gentle with the seeds, otherwise, they won't grow."

Mary took what the farmer said to heart and finally understood the importance of patience. She took her time planting the seeds, and as she watched them grow into beautiful plants, she felt a sense of accomplishment and satisfaction. From that day onwards, Mary tried to be more patient in everything she did. She took her time eating her meals, working on her homework, and even playing with her friends. She found that things were much more enjoyable when he didn't rush through them.

Patience is a virtue, and it can lead to many rewards in life. It may not be easy to slow down and take things one step at a time, but it is always worth it in the end.

In a small village nestled in the mountains, lived two best friends named Chelsea and Jane. They had been friends since they were children and did everything together. They would go on adventures in the forest, swim in the nearby river, and help each other with their daily chores.

One day, while they were out exploring the forest, they came across a beautiful, sparkling diamond. Chelsea, being the greedy person she was, suggested that they keep it for themselves and not tell anyone about it.

But Jane, being the kind and honest person she was, suggested that they give it to the village elder, who would know what to do with it.

Chelsea, not wanting to lose the diamond, got angry with Jane and they had a falling out. They stopped speaking to each other and went their separate ways.

As time passed, Chelsea became increasingly lonely and realized that she had made a huge mistake. She missed her best friend and the enjoyable times they had shared. She knew that she needed to make things right and went to apologize to Jane.

Jane, being the forgiving person she was, forgave her and they became friends again. They returned the diamond to the village elder, who was overjoyed and thanked them for their honesty by later awarding them with plaques at a public ceremony.

Chelsea and Jane were closer than ever and they knew that their friendship would last a lifetime. They learned that true friendship is built on trust, honesty, and forgiveness.

Located in the heart of a remote town, a young woman named Isabella resided and spent her days tending to her garden and caring for her elderly parents. Although she was content with her simple life, Isabella couldn't help but feel a sense of longing for something more in life.

One afternoon, while out for a walk in the forest, she stumbled upon a handsome young man named Adrian, who was lost and in need of assistance. Isabella kindly offered to help him find his way back to his town which neighbored hers. As they walked and talked, Isabella couldn't help but feel a spark of attraction towards Adrian.

Over the next few days, Adrian visited Isabella frequently, and their friendship quickly blossomed into love. They spent their days exploring the forest and sharing their dreams and hopes for the future.

As their love grew stronger, so did the disapproval of Isabella's parents. They believed that Adrian, who was from a wealthy and influential family, was not suitable for their daughter. Despite their objections, Isabella knew in her heart that Adrian was the one she wanted to spend the rest of her life with.

With the support of her friends, Isabella and Adrian were able to convince her parents of their true love. They eventually got married in a beautiful ceremony in the city center, surrounded by their loved ones. As they stood together, hand in hand, Isabella couldn't help but feel grateful for the day she stumbled upon the lost and handsome stranger in the town, who would become the love of her life. From that day on, they lived happily ever after.

A kind and generous man named Raj lived in a small town. He was well-liked by all in the town for his selfless acts of kindness, as he would often give food to the poor and help those in need without expecting anything in return.

A rich and selfish businessman named Vikram later moved to the town, was rude to the villagers, and only cared about making more money. He would often cheat and deceive people to get what he wanted.

As time passed, Raj's kindness and generosity brought him great wealth and success, while Vikram's selfishness and deceit led to his downfall. The locals saw this as the result of karma, the principle that good actions lead to good consequences, and bad actions lead to bad consequences.

Vikram realized the error of his ways and begged Raj for forgiveness. Raj, being the kind person he was, forgave Vikram and taught him the ways of kindness and generosity. From then on, Vikram's life changed for the better and he too was able to achieve wealth and success through good deeds.

The villagers were happy to see that karma had brought justice and that both Raj and Vikram were now successful and respected members of the community. They all lived happily ever after, knowing that the law of karma was always at work in their lives.

There was a boy from Saga Prefecture in Japan named Shun who was determined to become a professional athlete but had one major obstacle: he was born with a limp. Despite this setback, Shun refused to let his disability define him and was determined to achieve his dream.

He would wake up early every morning and spend hours training, pushing himself to be better but faced many challenges and obstacles, however, he never gave up. Shun's perseverance and determination paid off when he was offered a scholarship to a top sports university.

At university, Shun faced new challenges as he was competing against athletes who were not only more physically gifted, but also had more resources and opportunities. Nonetheless, Shun refused to let that discourage him and continued to work hard.

Finally, his hard work paid off when he made the school's varsity team, and even became the team's captain. He went on to have a successful college career and got a chance to play professionally in the domestic league.

Shun's story of perseverance inspired many, and his determination to overcome his obstacles and achieve his dream became a source of inspiration for others facing challenges. He proved that with hard work, dedication, and perseverance, anyone can achieve their goals and overcome any obstacle that comes their way.

Ambitious Peter had big dreams for the future. One thing he could not shake was that he often found himself wasting time on things that didn't matter, like scrolling through social media or playing video games.

Peter realized that the time he was wasting could be used to achieve his goals. He made a detailed plan to use his time more efficiently and set specific goals for himself by making a schedule to keep himself on track and accountable.

It was difficult at first for Peter to stick to his plan. He found himself slipping back into old habits and wasting time again. He battled his demons and with determination and discipline, he was able to overcome his temptations. He began making progress toward his goals, and before long, he was able to accomplish things he never thought possible.

Peter's story serves as a reminder that time is precious and should not be wasted. It also shows that with the right mindset and a plan of action, anyone can overcome their bad habits and achieve their dreams. Time is money and we cannot get an hour back.

Two working parents had a young boy named Dale who was not an easy child to raise. He often complained about everything from the food his mother cooked to the clothes his father bought him. He took everything for granted and never seemed to be grateful for anything. Dale's parents decided that it was time for him to learn a lesson about gratitude. They told him that he would have to spend a week living with a poor family in the countryside. Dale was not happy about this, but he had no choice but to go. When he arrived at the family's small, run-down house, he was greeted by a mother, father, and their five children. They were all very kind to him, but Dale could not help but notice how different their life was from his own. They had very little money and lived in a one-room house with no electricity or running water. Despite this, Dale soon realized that the family was happy and content. They had each other and were grateful for the simple things in life, like a warm meal and a comfortable bed. Dale began to see how much he had taken for granted and how little he had truly appreciated.

Over the week, Dale helped the family with their chores and even made friends with the children. He realized that the things he used to complain about were not important and that there were many things in his own life that he should be grateful for. When he returned home, Dale was a changed boy. He appreciated everything his parents did for him and no longer took anything for granted. He was grateful for the simple things in life and knew that true happiness came from being content with what you have. From then on, Dale's life was filled with joy and gratitude. He was a kinder and more appreciative person, and his family and friends couldn't be happier about the change in him. He had learned the true meaning of gratitude.

John was very successful in his career having a high-paying job, a beautiful home, and all the latest gadgets. Despite his success, John was not a happy person. He was arrogant and believed that he was better than everyone else. He would often look down on people and make them feel small.

John went on a business trip and stayed at a small inn. The innkeeper, who was a kind and humble man, took an interest in John and asked him about his life. John, thinking that the innkeeper was beneath him, shrugged off the conversation and went to bed. That night, John had a dream. In the dream, he was in a dark and gloomy place, and he was all alone. Suddenly, he heard a voice calling out to him. The voice said, "John, look at your life. You have everything you could ever want, but you are not happy. You are arrogant and believe that you are better than everyone else. This is not the way to live. You must learn humility."

John awoke the next morning, feeling different. He realized that the innkeeper had been trying to teach him about humility. He felt ashamed of his behavior and knew that he needed to change. He apologized to the innkeeper and thanked him for his wisdom. From that day on, John made a conscious effort to be humble. He began to treat people with kindness and respect, and he found that his relationships improved. He also found that he was happier and more fulfilled. In the end, John realized that true success is not measured by material possessions, but by the way one treats others. John's story serves as a reminder that humility is the key to true happiness, and that material possessions do not bring true success.

Mark grew up in a country where money was scarce and bartering was the norm. As he grew older, he became determined to find a way to make more money, so he set out on a journey to the big city to seek his fortune.

When he arrived, he discovered that money was the key to success in the city. He quickly learned that the more money he had, the more opportunities he had to improve his life. He worked hard, saved his money, and soon had enough to start his own business.

As his business grew, so did his wealth. He became one of the wealthiest men in the city, and with his newfound wealth, he was able to help those in his village who were still struggling. He built schools and hospitals and provided jobs for the people in his village.

But as time passed, Mark discovered that money could not buy happiness. He had everything he wanted but still felt empty inside. He realized that true happiness comes from helping others and making a difference in the world.

In the end, Mark used his wealth to make a difference in the lives of many, and he lived a life of fulfillment and purpose. He understood that money is important, but it is not the most important thing in life.

Emily fell deeply in love with a man named Thomas, and they had a beautiful relationship filled with laughter and love.

Thomas one day suddenly ended things with Emily without any explanation. She was devastated and couldn't understand why he would throw away their love so easily.

She tried to move on, but the pain of the heartbreak was overwhelming. She couldn't eat or sleep, and the thought of him consumed her every waking moment.

She reached out to him, but he refused to speak to her or even acknowledge her existence. She felt lost and alone as if a part of her had been ripped away.

As time went on, Emily slowly started to heal. She realized that she deserved better than someone who could so easily throw away their love. She started to focus on herself, and eventually, she met someone new who loved and appreciated her for who she was.

Even though she had moved on, the memory of Thomas and the heartbreak he caused her still lingered. She realized that heartbreak is a part of life, but it's also a part of growing and learning to love again.

Emily learned to trust her instincts and never settle for less than she deserved. Grateful for the experience, as it taught her to never take love for granted and to always cherish it when she had it.

A young woman named Sarah was constantly stressed out, worked long hours at her job as a marketing manager, and always felt like she had too much to do and not enough time to do it.

Despite her best efforts, Sarah couldn't shake the feeling of being overwhelmed, found herself snapping at her friends and family, and struggling to sleep at night. She knew she needed to find a way to manage her stress, but wasn't sure where to start.

Sarah decided to talk to her doctor about her stress. Her doctor suggested that she try practicing mindfulness meditation, and gave her a list of apps and resources to help her get started. Sarah was hesitant at first but decided to give it a try. She downloaded a meditation app and started practicing mindfulness for just a few minutes each day. At first, it was difficult for her to quiet her mind and focus on the present moment, but she persisted.

Over time, Sarah began to notice a change in her stress levels. She found that she was able to stay calm and focused even when she was faced with challenging situations at work. She also started sleeping better and found that she was able to be more patient and understanding with her friends and family.

Sarah realized that mindfulness meditation had helped her to develop a new perspective on stress. Instead of feeling like a victim of her stress, she now felt like she had the power to manage it. She continued to practice mindfulness regularly, and it became an important part of her daily routine. With the help of mindfulness, Sarah was able to overcome her stress and start living a happier, more balanced life.

Ian always dreamed of becoming a successful businessperson. He worked hard and saved every penny he could, eventually saving enough to start his own company however, things did not go as planned. Ian's business failed miserably and he was left with a mountain of debt and no income, feeling devastated and felt like a complete failure.

Ian refused to give up. He realized that failure was simply a learning experience and decided to pick himself back up and try again by taking a job as a salesperson to gain more experience and eventually worked his way up to becoming a manager.

Years passed, and Ian never gave up on his dream of starting his own business. He continued to work hard and save money, and eventually, he had enough to start a new company. This time, he was more prepared and made sure to thoroughly research the market and competition.

To his delight, the new company was a huge success. Ian's determination and willingness to learn from his mistakes had paid off. He was now a successful businessman and proud of the journey that led him there.

From that day on, Ian always remembered the lessons he learned from his failure and used them to become even more successful. He knew that failure was not the end, but simply a stepping stone to success.

Domiciled in a big city, Zomi was thought to be kind, and hardworking, had many friends, however, she also had a problem with jealousy. She couldn't help but feel envious of her friends' successes and possessions.

Zomi's best friend, Yui, came to her with exciting news. Yui had just been offered a scholarship to study abroad, something that Zomi had always dreamed of doing. Instead of being happy for her friend, Zomi felt a wave of jealousy wash over her. She couldn't understand why Yui deserved such an opportunity, and not her. Feeling guilty about her jealousy, Zomi decided to talk to her wise old grandmother. Her grandmother listened patiently as Emily poured out her feelings of envy and resentment.

"Child," her grandmother said, "jealousy is a poison that will only harm you in the end. It will make you unhappy and will cause you to push away those you love. You must learn to let go of your envy and be happy for others' successes."

Zomi didn't understand what her grandmother meant until Yui's departure day when she saw the excitement and joy on Yui's face as she hugged her goodbye and wished her the best. Zomi realized that her jealousy had not only been unfair to Yui, but it had also been stealing her happiness.

From that day on, Zomi made a conscious effort to let go of her jealousy. She celebrated her friends' accomplishments, and they, in turn, celebrated hers. She found that by doing so, she was able to build stronger and more meaningful relationships with those around her. She also found that her happiness and success increased as well. And so, Zomi learned that jealousy is wrong and that true happiness is found in loving and supporting others.

Jenny had always been a dreamer, constantly looking for new experiences and adventures. Be as it may, as she grew older, she began to realize that she had not taken full advantage of her youth and had missed out on many opportunities and became filled with regret for all the things she had not done and all the chances she had missed. One day in particular, Jenny decided that she would no longer live with regrets, promising herself that she would live her life to the fullest and make the most of every opportunity that came her way. She would then quit her job, sold her house, and bought a one-way ticket to travel the world.

Jenny traveled to different countries, experiencing new cultures and meeting new people, hiked through the mountains, swam in the ocean, and even bungee-jumped off a bridge. She took risks and put herself out of her comfort zone, and in doing so, she found a sense of freedom and fulfillment that she had never known before.

Through her journey, Jenny discovered that living without regrets is not about never making mistakes, but about learning from them and using them to grow and improve, learned that true happiness comes from living in the moment and embracing life's uncertainties. Eventually, Jenny returned home and decided to start a new chapter in her life by enrolling in school and becoming a travel writer, sharing her stories and experiences with others, and inspiring them to also live life without regrets. Jenny from that point on lived her life to the fullest and never looked back with regret knew that every experience, good or bad, was a valuable lesson and she was grateful for every one of them. She passed away late in life happy, contented, and with no regrets.

In a remote area within the Mid-West of America, lived a young girl named Maya who was born with a rare gift, the ability to hear music in everything. The rustling of the leaves, the chirping of the birds, and even the sound of the wind, all held a melody for her.

Maya spent her days listening to the music of the world around her and singing her songs. She was always happiest when she was singing and playing her flute and her music was so beautiful that it could bring tears to the eyes of those who heard it.

A terrible drought had struck the city she resided in, and all the crops began to wither and die. The residents and farmers were afraid that they would not have enough food to survive the winter. Maya knew that she had to do something to help her people, so she went to the top of the mountain to play her flute and ask the spirits of the wind to bring rain.

For three days and three nights, Maya played her flute, and on the fourth day, the skies opened, and the rain poured down. The town was saved, and the crops were able to grow again.

From that day on, the locals knew that Maya's music was a powerful force, and they would always turn to her in times of trouble or despair, as her music had the power to heal their hearts and bring them hope.

Maya continued to play her flute and sing her songs for many years onwards, and her music brought joy and peace to the town, Even when she passed on, her music lived on, a reminder of the power of music to bring people together and to heal the world.

In a far-off land, there was a beautiful forest that was home to many different kinds of animals and plants. The people who lived near the forest loved it and took great care to protect it, for they knew that it was a precious resource that needed to be preserved for future generations.

A day would come when a group of loggers came to the forest and began cutting down trees to make room for a new housing development. The people who lived near the forest were outraged and knew that they had to act fast to save their beloved forest.

They rallied together and formed a group called "The Forest Protectors." Their goal was to raise awareness about the importance of protecting the environment and stopping the loggers from destroying the forest.

The Forest Protectors organized a peaceful protest and marched to the logging site, holding signs that read "Save Our Forest" and "Nature is Our Heritage." They also contacted local media outlets to share their message and gain support from the community.

Their efforts paid off in the end, as more and more people began to realize the importance of protecting the environment. The logging company was forced to halt its operations, and the Forest Protectors were able to work with the government to create a plan for preserving the forest and its wildlife.

The forest was saved, and it remains a beautiful and thriving ecosystem to this day. The people who live near the forest continue to take great care to protect it, and they are proud to have played a part in preserving it for future generations.

When people come together to protect the environment, they can make a real difference. It's important to take action to protect our natural resources and preserve them for future generations.

Nicole loved spending her free time on social media, playing video games, and scrolling through Instagram and Twitter. She enjoyed connecting with her friends and family, sharing her photos and thoughts, and escaping into her favorite virtual worlds. As time went on, Nicole began to realize that her excessive use of technology was hurting her life. She found herself becoming more and more isolated, spending less time interacting with the people around her and more time staring at her phone or computer screen. She also noticed that her mood and self-esteem were suffering, as she constantly compared herself to the seemingly perfect lives of others on social media.

Despite these negative effects, Nicole couldn't help but feel addicted to her digital devices and the instant gratification they provided. She knew she needed to make a change, but didn't know how to break the cycle, so she decided to take a break from social media and video games, and instead focus on building real-life relationships and hobbies. She picked up a volunteering gig at a local shelter, took up photography as a hobby, and reconnected with old friends. She soon discovered the benefits of offline social interactions and started to develop a sense of self-worth that wasn't based on likes or followers.

Nicole realized that while social media, Instagram, Twitter, and video games can be great sources of entertainment and connection, they should not consume our lives taking into consideration that It's important to use technology in moderation but to make sure to maintain a balance between our online and offline activities, to improve our mental and physical well-being. From then on, Nicole made sure to use social media, play video games and spend time on Instagram and Twitter in moderation, and always make sure to prioritize her offline interactions and activities.

Art is interesting because it allows us to express ourselves in ways that words cannot. It gives us the freedom to explore our imagination and emotions and to communicate them to others. It also allows us to connect with others by sharing our experiences and perspectives. Additionally, art can be used to explore important social and political issues and to challenge our understanding of the world. It can also be aesthetically pleasing or evoke strong emotions or memories. Overall, art is interesting because it allows for endless possibilities of self-expression and interpretation.

Art has always been a part of human culture, and it continues to play an important role in our lives today. For many of us, art is a source of inspiration and a way to express ourselves. It can be a form of self-discovery, helping us to understand our thoughts and emotions.

Art can also be a form of escape, allowing us to lose ourselves in a painting, sculpture, or film. It can take us on a journey to faraway places, introduce us to new cultures, and even transport us back in time.

Art can also be a powerful tool for social and political change. Throughout history, artists have used their work to raise awareness about important issues and inspire people to take action.

In addition, art can be a source of great pleasure and enjoyment. Whether we are creating it ourselves or admiring the work of others, art can bring us joy and happiness.

Overall, art is an essential part of the human experience, and it has the power to inspire, educate, and entertain us. It is no wonder that art is so interesting to us.

Patrick lived in a tiny dwelling at the foot of a mountain. was an ambitious boy who dreamed of one day climbing the mountain and seeing what lay beyond. In spite of his hopes, Patrick was not just any ordinary boy, he was also incredibly unlucky. Patrick decided that he would finally take his chance and climb the mountain, packed his bag with food, and water, and put on his hiking boots, to set off on his journey, but as soon as he started climbing, his luck seemed to take a turn for the worse.

First, he slipped on a loose rock and twisted his ankle. Then, it started to rain and he got soaked to the bone. As he trudged on, he encountered a swarm of mosquitoes that refused to leave him alone. Just as he thought things couldn't get any worse, he got lost in the thick fog that had rolled in. Feeling defeated, Patrick decided to turn back and head home, however as he was making his way down the mountain, he stumbled upon a small cave. Inside, where he found a warm fire, a comfortable bed, and a mysterious old man who offered him shelter.

The old man listened to Patrick's story and then told him that luck was not something that could be controlled or predicted. He explained that it was not luck that had led Patrick to the cave, but his determination and persistence.

Patrick stayed in the cave for the night and the next day, he felt refreshed and ready to continue his journey. He thanked the old man and set off on his climb once more. This time, his luck seemed to change. The sun came out, the fog lifted, and he found his way back home safely.

Patrick from that point no longer believed in luck. He knew that it was his determination and hard work that would guide him to success, and sure enough, he eventually reached the summit of the mountain and saw the beautiful view that lay beyond.

Humans are incredibly similar to one another, despite our many differences in terms of culture, language, and appearance. At the most basic level, all humans share the same genetic code, which determines everything from the color of our eyes to the shape of our bones. This genetic code is 99.9% identical from person to person, meaning that we are all more alike than we are different.

Additionally, humans have a wide range of common behaviors and experiences, including the ability to feel emotions, form relationships, and communicate with one another. Even though we may have different cultural backgrounds and speak different languages, we all share a common humanity that connects us.

Scientists have also found that humans have a lot of similar physical characteristics, such as body proportions, and the way we walk, run and move.

Overall, the similarities between humans far outweigh the differences, and it is this shared humanity that allows us to connect and empathize with one another.

Cecile loved playing basketball, playing since she was five years old and had become quite skilled at it but one day, during a game in her high school's championship, she sprained her ankle sitting out for the rest of the season.

Cecile was devastated impart that she had been working towards this moment for years and now it was all gone. On the other hand, her coach, who saw her potential, told her that this was not the end of her basketball career. He said, "Cecile, you can bounce back from this. You just need to have faith in yourself and work hard." Those words stuck with her and she began to work hard to recover from her injury. She went to physical therapy, worked out on her own, and even practiced her shooting and ball handling while sitting down, determined to come back stronger than ever.

Months passed and her ankle had fully healed. Where she returned to her high school team, and they were able to win the state championship. Cecile was named MVP of the championship game, scoring the most points on the team.

After that impressive performance, she received a scholarship to play college basketball and went on to play professionally, becoming one of the best players in the league and even earned the nickname "Bounce Back" for her ability to overcome adversity.

Cecile never forgot her coach's words and always remembered to have faith in herself and to work hard. She knew that anything was possible if she put her mind to it and that she could always bounce back from any setback.

Andy was a happy child, always laughing and playing with his friends however one day, tragedy struck when Andy's parents were killed in a car accident. Andy was left alone and had to go live with his aunt and uncle who lived in the city, heartbroken he didn't understand why this had happened to him. He missed his parents dearly and felt like a piece of his heart was missing.

His aunt and uncle did their best to take care of him, but they were busy with their own lives and didn't have much time to spend with him. Andy felt lonely and isolated in the city, and he struggled to make friends at school. Years passed, and Andy grew up where he finished high school and decided to go back to his old stomping grounds, the place where he had grown up and where his parents were buried because he wanted to be close to them and the memories, he had of them.

When he arrived, he found that the landscape had changed. Many new people had moved in and there were new houses and buildings everywhere, nonetheless what caught his eye was a small community center that had been built in the center of the town. He went inside and found that it was a place where people of all ages could come to play games, read books, and take classes. Andy was amazed by how much the village had changed and how much better it was for everyone. He then realized that this was his parents' legacy, they had been the ones who had started the project and never got to see it finished but it was now completed for the good of the town.

Andy felt a sense of happiness and contentment that he had never felt before, as he knew that his parents were still with him in spirit and that they would always be a part of his life. He made friends with the other people in the town and started volunteering at the community center, helping to organize events and classes. Andy finally found his place in the world and felt like he belonged, knowing that his parents would be proud of him, he was happy to make a difference in his hometown, just like they had.

There was a small town called Prosperity, where the economy was thriving. The businesses were doing well, the unemployment rate was low, and people were generally happy. However, one day a large factory, which was the main employer in the town, announced that it was closing its doors and moving to another state.

The people of Prosperity were shocked and saddened by the news. Many of them had worked at the factory for years and now they were out of a job. The closure of the factory also had a ripple effect on the other businesses in the town, as people had less money to spend and many of them had to close as well. The unemployment rate skyrocketed, and many people were struggling to make ends meet. The once-thriving town was now in a state of recession, and it seemed like there was no way out.

Despite this, the people of Prosperity were determined to bounce back and came together and formed a task force to come up with a plan to revive the economy. They invited experts from different fields to come and share their ideas, and they also sought out funding from the government to help them get started. They came up with a plan to attract new businesses to the town, by offering tax breaks and other incentives. They also started a campaign to promote the town as a tourist destination. They organized festivals and events, and they created a website to showcase all the wonderful things Prosperity had to offer.

Their efforts paid off, and new businesses started to open up in the town. The unemployment rate began to drop, and people were starting to find jobs again. The economy was slowly but surely recovering. The people of Prosperity were proud of what they had accomplished. They had shown that even in the face of adversity, they could come together and make a difference. They had turned a struggling town into a thriving community once again, proving that the economy is a constantly evolving thing that can be shaped and molded by the actions and decisions of its inhabitants.

Gentle and compassionate in nature Amy had a gift for listening and truly understanding the problems and concerns of those around her.

A new family moved into the township and they were having a difficult time adjusting. Amy noticed that the mother, who had recently given birth, seemed particularly down, so she went to visit the family and asked if there was anything she could do to help.

The mother opened up to Amy and shared that she was struggling with postpartum depression and feeling isolated in their new surroundings. Amy listened attentively, nodding and offering words of encouragement, then suggested that they set up a weekly playdate for their children, so the mother could have some adult company and the opportunity to form new friendships.

The mother was grateful for Amy's understanding and support and over time, the playdates became a regular occurrence and the mother's mood improved significantly. Amy's act of being a good listener not only helped the mother but also the entire family and the community.

People soon realized the value of Amy's listening skills and began to seek her out when they needed someone to talk to. Amy's ability to listen without judgment or interruption made her an invaluable member of the community. She had become a true friend and confidant to many.

From that day forward, the township was a happier and more connected place, all because of one woman's simple act of being a good listener.

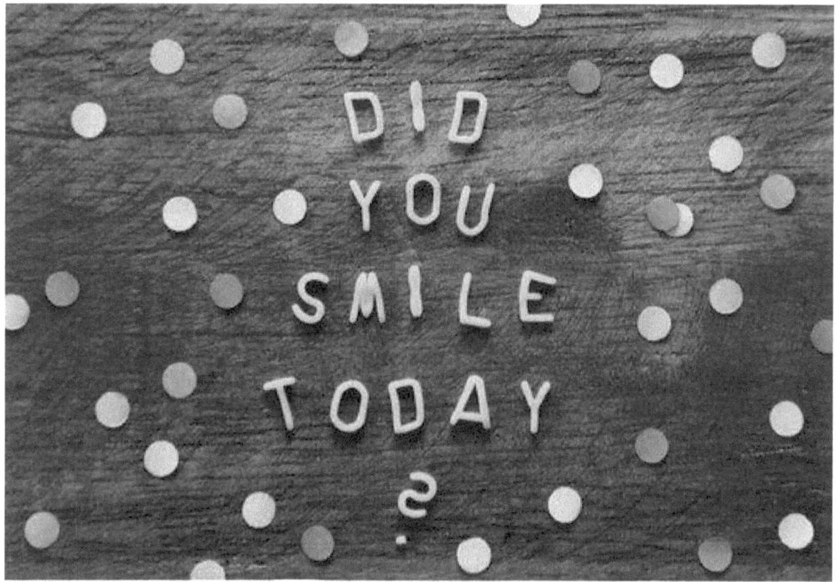

Kate had always prided herself on being disciplined and responsible in all aspects of her life. She worked hard at her job as a lawyer, exercised regularly, and ate a healthy diet, but despite her best efforts, Sarah had a secret guilty pleasure that she couldn't resist: junk food.

Whenever she was feeling stressed or down, Kate would sneak away to the nearest convenience store and stock up on her favorite treats: chocolate bars, chips, and soda. She would devour them in the privacy of her own home, savoring every bite while feeling a sense of guilty pleasure wash over her.

Kate knew that her junk food habit was bad for her health, and she tried to resist it on many occasions. But no matter how hard she tried, she couldn't shake the cravings. She felt like a prisoner to her desires, and the guilt weighed heavily on her.

Kate decided that enough was enough. She knew that she needed to take control of her guilty pleasure and find a way to enjoy it in moderation. She started by setting strict limits for herself: only allowing herself to indulge in junk food once a week, and always in small portions.

At first, it was difficult for Kate to stick to her new routine. But over time, she found that she was able to enjoy her guilty pleasure without feeling guilty and discovered that it was possible to indulge in the things she loved without letting them control her life. In the end, Kate learned that a little bit of what you love can be a good thing, as long as you keep it in balance.

There was a wealthy businessman named Grant who built his fortune through ruthless deals and cutthroat tactics, never satisfied with what he had. His greed consumed him, driving him to always want more, no matter the cost.

Grant heard about a small village on the outskirts of town that was rich in natural resources and without hesitation, he set out to buy the land and exploit its resources for his gain. He offered the villagers a small sum of money, but they refused, saying that the land had been in their family for generations and they could never part with it.

Undeterred, Grant began to use underhanded methods to try and force the villagers to sell. He bribed officials, spread rumors, and even threatened violence, but the villagers stood strong, refusing to be pushed around by a greedy businessman.

As time passed, Grant's obsession with the village grew. He spent all of his time and money trying to acquire it, neglecting his business and his family. His once-loving wife left him, and his children disowned him. Even as his life fell apart, Grant couldn't let go of his greed, as he continued to scheme and plot, determined to have the village at any cost.

Finally, the villagers had had enough. They banded together and chased Grant out of town, warning him never to return.

Shamed and alone, Grant realized too late the true cost of his greed. He had lost everything that was once important to him and gained nothing but emptiness. He wandered the earth, a lonely and pitied figure, a cautionary tale of the dangers of giving in to greed.

Angela's sympathetic and soft-hearted nature was due to her special bond with her grandmother, who taught her the importance of forgiveness.

A spring afternoon, while Angela was playing in the nearby park, she saw a group of children teasing a new boy in town. They were making fun of his clothes and the way he talked. Angela felt a pang of sadness for the boy and knew she had to do something to help.

She walked up to the group and asked them to stop, telling them that everyone deserved to be treated with kindness and respect, no matter how different they may seem. The children were taken aback by Angela's words and realized the error of their ways. They apologized to the boy and became friends with him.

News of Angela's kindness spread throughout the neighborhood, and she became known as a peacemaker.

Years passed, and Angela grew up to be a wise and respected leader in her neighborhood. One day, an old enemy of the area returned, seeking forgiveness for the harm they had caused. The people in the neighborhood were hesitant to forgive, but Angela reminded them of the lessons her grandmother had taught her and urged them to find it in their hearts to forgive.

With Angela's guidance, the people were able to forgive the enemy and welcome them back into the community. Peace and prosperity returned to the neighborhood, and Angela's name was remembered for generations as a symbol of forgiveness and understanding.

Angela's actions taught them that forgiveness is not always easy, but it is always worth it. It can bring healing and peace to those who give and receive it.

Christopher felt lost and unsure of his purpose in life and often went through days feeling unfulfilled and uninspired, constantly searching for something that would give their life meaning.

Christopher decided to take a long walk in the countryside to clear their mind and try to find some answers. As he walked, he came across an old, abandoned farm. Intrigued, he decided to explore the property. As he walked around the farm, he noticed that the fields were overgrown and the buildings were in disrepair.

Christopher came to a sudden realization - this farm could be his purpose. He could restore the farm to its former glory and create a sustainable, self-sufficient life for himself and the people who would need to use the farm. Excited by this new idea, they immediately got to work.

Over the next few months, Christopher worked tirelessly to clear the fields, repair the buildings, and plant crops. They also began to raise animals and started building a community of like-minded individuals who shared their vision of sustainable living.

As the farm began to flourish, Christopher finally felt a sense of purpose and fulfillment that he had never experienced before, realizing that their true purpose in life was to use their skills and passions to make a positive impact on the world and help others.

Christopher later devoted his life to continuing growth and improving the farm, helping others to find their purpose, and creating a more sustainable world for future generations.

In a far-off land, there lived a king who believed that beauty was the most important thing in the world. He had a huge castle and many fine things, but he was always searching for the most beautiful person in the land to be his queen. The king sent out messengers to every village and town, asking people to come to his castle to be judged on their beauty. Many people came, but none were deemed beautiful enough to be the king's queen. One day, a poor farmer named Tom decided to try his luck. He was not particularly handsome, and his clothes were old and worn, but he had a kind heart and a generous spirit. When he arrived at the castle, the king scoffed at him and told him to leave.

But Tom refused to go. He told the king that beauty came in many forms, and that true beauty was found in the heart, not in outward appearances. The king laughed at him, but Tom persisted. Finally, the king decided to give Jason a chance. He asked him to show him what true beauty was. Tom led the king out of the castle and into the countryside. They walked for miles until they came to a small village. There, they saw a group of children playing in the sunshine. They were dirty and ragged, but their faces were full of joy and laughter. The king was touched by their happiness, and he realized that Tom was right. Beauty was not just about looks, it was also about kindness, compassion, and joy.

The king would declare that all people were beautiful in their way, and he stopped searching for the most beautiful person in the land. He and Tom became friends, and the king invited the villagers to the castle to live with him, and they all lived happily ever after. True beauty lies in the heart and all people are beautiful in their unique way. Everyone should be seen and appreciated for who they truly are.

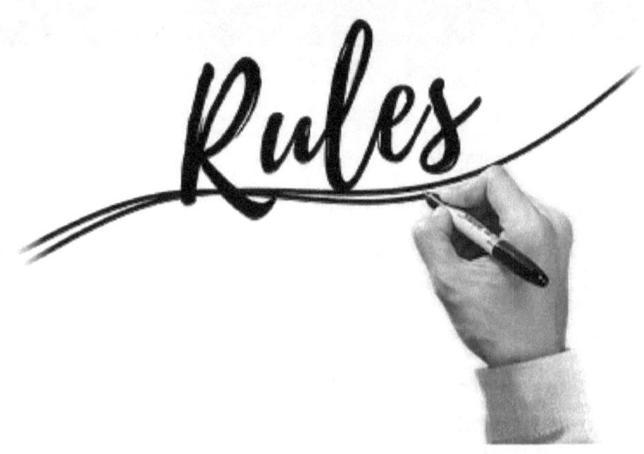

A group lived a peaceful and harmonious life in a shared house, however, one day, a group of outsiders came and took over the house, imposing strict rules on the roommates. The roommates were not allowed to gather in groups larger than three, speak out against outsiders, and they were not allowed to bring people into the house without permission.

At first, the roommates were afraid and complied with the rules, but as time went on, they began to realize that they were not living their best lives under these rules. They missed the days of freedom and community, and they knew that they had to do something to change their situation.

One boy named Dan came up with an idea, where he proposed that they create their own set of rules, rules that would allow them to live their lives as they wanted, without fear or oppression. The other roommates were hesitant at first, but as they heard Dan's idea, they began to see the wisdom in his words. Together, the roommates came up with a new set of rules. They decided that everyone would have the right to speak their minds, gather in groups larger than three, and they would be allowed to invite whoever they wanted to without permission.

The outsiders were furious when they heard about the new rules, but the roommates stood firm. They knew that these rules were necessary for their freedom and happiness, and they were not going to give them up. In the end, the outsiders were forced to leave the house, and the roommates were finally able to live their lives as they wanted. After that, they lived by their own rules and never looked back. Rules are important, but they must be created by the people they affect, and they must be fair and just. It's also important to question the rules imposed on us by others and to strive for freedom and autonomy.

Artificial intelligence (AI) has the potential to revolutionize many industries and improve our daily lives in countless ways. One major benefit of AI is its ability to process and analyze large amounts of data quickly and accurately, which can help make important decisions in fields like healthcare, finance, and transportation.

In healthcare, for example, AI can be used to analyze patient data and help doctors make more accurate diagnoses. AI-powered systems can also help identify patterns in large amounts of medical research, which can lead to new treatments and cures for diseases.

In finance, AI can be used to detect fraudulent activity, assess credit risk, and make trades in milliseconds. This can help financial institutions make better decisions and operate more efficiently.

In transportation, AI can help optimize routes for delivery trucks, reduce traffic congestion, and improve the safety of self-driving cars.

Another important application of AI is natural language processing (NLP), which enables computers to understand and generate human language. This can be used to improve customer service, automate mundane tasks, and even create new forms of entertainment.

Overall, the potential of AI is immense, and it is likely to have a profound impact on many aspects of our lives in the future.

Making a good impression and getting friends takes time and effort. Here is a story about a person who successfully made new friends:

Abby who moved to a new city for a job opportunity was feeling a bit nervous about making new friends in a new place, but she decided to take the initiative and put herself out there.

First, Abby joined a local gym and started going regularly. She made small talk with people during her workouts and even joined a group fitness class. This helped her meet new people who shared her interest in fitness.

Next, Abby joined a local book club through a community center. She found that the people in the book club were friendly and welcoming, and they had a lot in common. They bonded over their love of reading and even started meeting outside of the book club for coffee or lunch.

Abby also made an effort to be friendly and approachable in her new workplace. She went out of her way to introduce herself to her coworkers and even organized a team lunch to get to know everyone better.

By putting herself out there and being friendly and approachable, Abby was able to make new friends in her new city. It may take time and effort, but if you're willing to put yourself out there, you can make new friends as well.

Gary didn't pay much attention to his health, and would often skip breakfast and eat fast food for lunch and dinner. He rarely exercised and would often spend his days sitting in front of the computer.

As a result, Gary began to gain weight and feel sluggish, after having trouble sleeping at night and feeling tired during the day. He also started to develop health issues such as high blood pressure and high cholesterol. One day, Gary's doctor told him that if he didn't make some changes to his lifestyle, or face the risk of serious health problems in the future. The doctor recommended that Gary start exercising regularly and eating a healthy diet.

At first, Gary was resistant to the idea. He didn't like the thought of giving up his favorite foods and spending hours at the gym. But he knew he had to make a change if he wanted to improve his health. So, Gary made a plan to start exercising three times a week and to eat a diet that was high in fruits, vegetables, and lean protein. He also made a point to prepare his meals at home instead of eating fast food.

It wasn't easy at first, but Gary soon found that he enjoyed the feeling of being active and eating nutritious foods. He had more energy and was able to sleep better at night. His health issues also began to improve.

Gary realized that taking care of his body was not only important for his physical health but also for his mental well-being. He was happy that he made the decision to make a change and felt proud of himself for sticking with it.

From that day on, Gary made sure to make exercising and eating a healthy diet a regular part of his life. He knew it was important to take care of his body and that it was worth the effort.

Harry on a journey to discover the meaning of life, had always been fascinated by the stories of the alchemists, who were said to be able to turn lead into gold and discover the elixir of life.

Harry would come across an old alchemist who took him under his wing and taught him the ways of alchemy. The old alchemist showed him how to transform matter and how to read the signs in nature that pointed to the path of enlightenment.

As Harry practiced the art of alchemy, he began to realize that the true purpose of alchemy was not to turn lead into gold but to transform the lead of his soul into the gold of wisdom and understanding. He learned that the elixir of life was not a physical substance, but a state of mind that could be achieved through inner transformation.

Harry dedicated himself to becoming an alchemist, spending years studying and practicing, and eventually, he too was able to turn lead into gold and discover the elixir of life. He understood that alchemy is not just about changing matter, but about changing ourselves and the world around us.

And so, I must be like the alchemist, constantly seeking to transform myself and the world for the better.

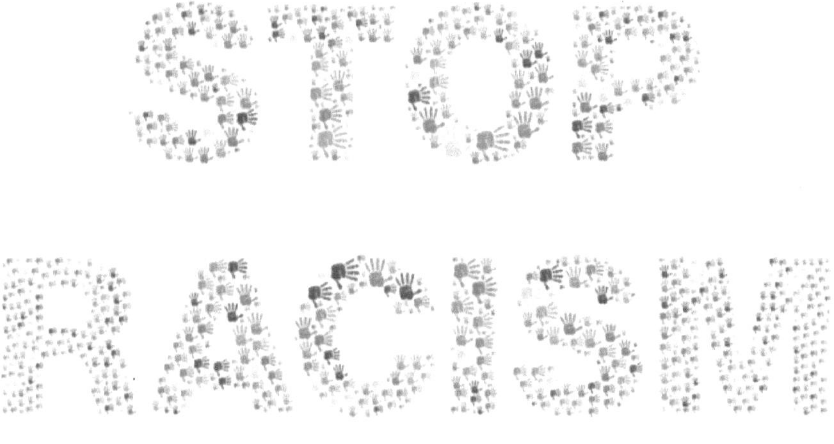

A humane and altruistic king ruled over his people with fairness and compassion. However, one day, a group of foreigners arrived in the town and the king's attitude towards them was different. He saw them as inferior and treated them with disdain and hostility.

The villagers, who had always looked up to their king as a role model, began to adopt his racist behavior and soon, the town was divided. The foreigners were not welcomed and were constantly bullied and mistreated by the natives.

A young girl from the town, who had always been taught to be kind and accepting of others, decided to take action. She made friends with one of the foreigners and through their interactions, she realized that they were not so different after all.

She shared her newfound understanding with her family and friends and soon, the entire town began to change. They apologized for their past behavior and worked to make amends. The king, too, recognized the error of his ways and made a public apology for his racist behavior.

The town was reunited and the foreigners were finally welcomed with open arms. The young girl's actions had taught them the importance of treating others with kindness and respect, regardless of their race or background. The town came to be known as a place of acceptance and diversity.

There was a group of women who loved to gossip, as they would spend hours sitting in the town square, discussing the latest news and rumors about their friends and neighbors.

A new woman moved into the village and the gossipers couldn't wait to get to know her. They invited her to join them in the town square, and she quickly became a regular member of their group.

However, the new woman had a secret. She was actually a witch, and she was able to cast spells with her words. She was tired of listening to the constant chatter and wanted to teach the gossipers a lesson.

As they sat in the square gossiping, the witch cast a spell on them. Suddenly, the women's words turned into birds that flew away into the sky. The gossipers were horrified and couldn't speak for days.

The women learned a valuable lesson about the power of words and how harmful gossip can be. Going forward, the women in the village were careful about what they said and made an effort to be kind and supportive of one another.

The witch, seeing the change in the village, lifted the spell and the women were able to speak again. They apologized to the witch and thanked her for teaching them the error of their ways.

The village became a peaceful and happy place, where everyone respected each other's privacy and avoided gossiping. The witch, no longer lonely, decided to stay in the village, and the village was a better place for it.

Vlad afraid of making mistakes would often avoid trying new things or taking on new challenges, and as a result, he missed out on many opportunities for growth and learning.

Vlad's teacher assigned the class a project to create a model of the solar system. Vlad was excited about the project, but also nervous about making mistakes. He was determined to create the best model, but he was so focused on not making mistakes that he became overwhelmed and didn't know where to start.

His classmates had already begun working on their models and were making progress, but Vlad was still staring at his blank project board, feeling lost.

Finally, he decided to take a break and went for a walk. As he was walking, he noticed a beautiful butterfly fluttering around a flower. The butterfly would fly to one flower, then another, and another, trying each one until it found the perfect one to land on.

Vlad realized that the butterfly was not afraid of making mistakes, it was just trying different things until it found the right one. And that is what he should do.

He went back to class and started working on his project with a new attitude, focusing on the process rather than the outcome. He made mistakes along the way, but he learned from them and kept trying.

In the end, Vlad's model of the solar system was not the best one in the class, but it was still a great project and he was proud of it. And he realized that the most important thing was not to avoid making mistakes but to learn from them and keep moving forward.

Vlad learned to accept and learn from his mistakes, he was no longer afraid of them, and he started to enjoy the process of trying new things. He found that the more he tried, the more he learned, and the more he grew.

Alex highly ambitious and driven was determined to be successful in all aspects of his life, so he worked tirelessly to achieve his goals.

As he began to climb the corporate ladder, Alex's ego grew with each promotion and success. He became increasingly self-centered and focused on his own success, often disregarding the needs and feelings of those around him.

Alex was given an important project to lead at work. He was determined to make it a success, and he threw himself into the work with all of his might. However, as the deadline approached, he realized that he had neglected the contributions of his team members and had not properly communicated his vision to them.

The project was a failure, and Alex was left feeling embarrassed and defeated. He realized that his ego had gotten in the way of his success and that he needed to learn to work with and listen to others if he wanted to truly succeed.

Alex made a conscious effort to check his ego and work collaboratively with others. He learned to value the perspectives and contributions of those around him and, as a result, was able to achieve even greater success than he had before.

Steve had a problem with addiction, always struggled with self-control, and had dabbled in drugs and alcohol throughout his teenage years, but it wasn't until he turned 21 that his problems with addiction truly began.

It started with just a few drinks at a party, but soon Steve was drinking every day. He would tell himself that he could stop at any time, but he never did. His drinking gradually got worse and worse, until he was unable to function without alcohol. He would drink in the morning to steady his nerves, and then continue drinking throughout the day.

His addiction not only affected him physically but also emotionally and mentally. He lost his job, so his friends and family were worried about him. He didn't know how to cope with the guilt and shame he felt, so he would drink even more.

He would eventually hit rock bottom, when he woke up in a hospital bed, not remembering how he got there. He realized that he needed help and he checked himself into rehab. It wasn't easy, but with the support of the staff and his family, he was able to overcome his addiction.

Steve learned how to cope with his emotions without turning to alcohol and he eventually got his life back on track. He would get a new job, reconnect with his family and friends, and was finally able to enjoy life without alcohol. He realized that addiction is a disease and it can happen to anyone. He dedicated himself to helping others overcome addiction, so they too can find a life of happiness and freedom.

In a small residential area located in the heart of a lush forest lived a kind and wise old man named Robert. Robert had lived there for many years and had seen the effects of pollution and waste on the beautiful forest that surrounded them.

One day, as he was walking through the forest, he came across a pile of discarded plastic bottles and cans littering the ground. This sight filled him with sadness, and he knew that he had to do something to protect the forest and its inhabitants.

That night, Robert had a dream in which the forest animals came to him, pleading with him to help them. They told him that the pollution and waste were harming their homes and making it difficult for them to survive.

Robert woke up determined to make a change. He knew that recycling was the key to protecting the forest and its inhabitants, so he set out to educate his neighbors about the importance of recycling and how it could help save the forest.

He began by setting up a recycling program in the area, where people could bring their waste to be sorted and properly disposed of. He also organized regular clean-up events to remove litter from the forest and the village. As the residents began to see the positive effects of recycling on the forest and its inhabitants, they too became more conscious of their waste and worked together to reduce it.

Over time, the area became known as a model for sustainable living, and other neighborhoods in the area began to follow their example. The forest was once again flourishing and the animals were happy and healthy.

Robert's dream of protecting the forest had become a reality, and he was grateful to have played a small part in preserving it for future generations.

There was a mountain in a rural town where the villagers had always been told that it was impossible to climb the towering peak that loomed over their homes. The mountain was said to be cursed and those who dared to climb it never returned, but there was one young man who refused to believe that something was impossible.

Mike was determined to reach the summit, being that he heard stories of the rich treasures that lay at the top of the mountain and he was determined to be the one to claim them. Mike spent months preparing for his climb. He trained his body to be strong and his mind to be determined. He readied supplies and equipment and set off on his journey.

The climb was treacherous and at times it seemed as if the mountain was trying to stop him, regardless Mike refused to give up. He pushed on through the blizzards and the high winds, always moving forward. Finally, after many long days of climbing, he reached the summit.

The villagers had said that the mountain was impossible to climb, but Mike had proven them wrong, doing the impossible and in doing so, he had shown that anything is possible if you have the will to make it happen.

Mike returned home to the village, a hero where he brought back with him the treasures he had found at the summit and shared them with the villagers. The villagers would now look at the mountain with new respect and many of them decided to climb it themselves, and they, too, discovered that with determination and hard work, they could accomplish the impossible.

Mike's legacy lived on, as the village became known for its adventurous spirit, and the people who lived there were no longer afraid to try new things and to push the boundaries of what is possible.

Lisa always seemed to find something to complain about, would grumble about the weather being too hot or too cold, about her food not being cooked just right, and about her toys not being as fun as she wanted them to be.

There would come a time when. her mother decided that enough was enough. She sat Lisa down and told her that she needed to start counting her blessings. "You have so many things to be thankful for," she said. "You have a roof over your head, food to eat, and toys to play with. There are many children in the world who don't have those things."

Lisa was a little skeptical at first, but she decided to give it a try. That night, before she went to bed, she sat down and made a list of all the things she was grateful for. She wrote down things like her family, her friends, her health, and her home. As she wrote, she began to feel a sense of warmth and happiness spreading through her. She realized that her mother was right - she did have so many things to be thankful for.

Lisa made it a habit to count her blessings every day. She would take a few minutes to reflect on all the good things in her life, and she found that it made her feel happier and more content.

As she grew older, she learned to appreciate the small things in life, like the beauty of a sunset or the sound of birds, singing. She also learned that by focusing on the positive, she was able to handle the negative things in life with more grace and resilience. In the end, counting her blessings became a cherished part of Lisa's daily routine and helped her to live a more fulfilled and joyful life.

9 7876 9 0537320